Sun And

By

David E. Pratt

Previous Publications:

'First Light.' © David E. Pratt 2018.
ISBN: 978-1-910693-76-6

First published in Great Britain in 2020 by Print2Demand Ltd

ISBN: 978-1-910693-28-5

All Rights Reserved.

© David E. Pratt 2020.

David E. Pratt is hereby identified as author of this work in accordance with Section 77 of the Copyright, Designs and Patents Act 1988.

No part of this publication may be reproduced in any form, by photocopying or by any electronic means, including information storage or retrieval systems, without permission in writing from both the copyright owner and the publisher of this book.

Printed in Great Britain by Print2Demand, Westoning, Bedfordshire.

To Beverley, Emma & Lisa and to Mum & Dad.

Forward

I studied at Manchester University, although Literature was not my chosen subject. However in leisure periods, I mixed and wrote with friends studying English who were writers to-be and gave me much encouragement to continue to write poetry.

At this time, the Manchester-based, Carcanet Press were publishing the works of C.H. Sisson, Michael Hamburger and Michael Schmidt, amongst others, which were a large influence on my writing.

Moving to London various poems were published in magazines such as Counterpoint and Wayfarers.

'Garden' was awarded the National Poetry Society's poem of the month, judged by Alan Brownjohn.

Now long settled in Bedforshire, I have continued writing and developing further ideas, some more in a lighter mood and with homage to EE Cummings, Roger McGough and even Splike Milligan.

'To see a world in a grain of sand'

William Blake
Auguries of Innocence

Contents

Pastures
Ants 1
Birds 2
Trees 3
Robin 4
Orchard 5
Bee Song 6
Hide 7

Places
Capital 8
Clouds 9
40 Nights 10
Keep 11
Garden 12
Pylon 13
Awakening 14
Computer-Crash 15
December 16

Homes
Bicycle 17
Father 18
Cake 19
Mother 20
Twins 21
Fireworks I 22
Fireworks II 23
Alfie 24
Mosaic 25

Hearts

Passengers 26
Perfume 27
Beach 28
Dissection 29
Gallery 30
Celebration 31
Not Gone 32
Rage 33
Shadow 34

Pastimes

Just A Game 35
Christmas Party 36
Typewriter 37
Backstage 38
Eight Thoughts 39
Planet 40
Choices 41

Histories

Bladud 42
Suspension 43
Surveyor 44
Money-lender 45
Tribute 46
Trenchman 47
Sarcophagus 48
Churchyard 49
Remembered 50

Ants

We lift the slab and let it fall,
finding them in millions
like filings under nature's magnet
they flow along arteries in the earth.

Sunlight crazes them to fast streams,
their banks hold under our shadow
hypnotized by their workings,
the silence of perfect machinery.

Each day they feel the giant's step
pressing on their avenues and caves,
packed with eggs like rice, becoming
accustomed, as a neighbour does.

When summer's heat bleeds them out
we watch one crack and smoulder
under a piece of glass. His pain
is small enough for us to bear.

Their unfamiliar size first amazed us,
then grew to concern, until we soon
feared them in numbers. I once read
to cross water they use leaves for boats.

Birds

Do not look
over our heads
as littered paper
lifted to sky
they leave this earth.

Shadows grouping
as mercury
into form
or order
as we would.

Habit draws them
to hot lands
bleached to white
the dust of ancestors.

Descending unwise
for already
the sun is spent
and chills them
in the silence of snow.

But we are here
denied wings,
staring unmoved
and do not see
the first fall of winter.

Trees

They lean stark and naked in winter
until summer's heat
ripens red fruit on each new day.

Concentric rings echo outwards
hearts of oak,
beat under walls of knotted skin.

The ripples circle outwards
until by degrees,
their annual maps are finished.

Children will dance round and
birds will roost
on branches unyielding to harsh winds.

In a hundred years their time comes,
sap dries to pulp
and gnarled roots curl to an angry fist.

Robin

Feathering friend
soil hopper

pedlar of seed
prince of winter-chill

spy in the twig
creation rejected

and ejected
a breast wound

on autumn brown
tilt head still

and small stare
a snick of omen.

Orchard

Swaying over a grey mist, beckoning
me to visit, a mile or two no more,
to the orchard, I came
stamping down bindweed and nettle
with young shoes wet, gleaming
in long grass furred with dew
and cold air knifing my throat.

Weaving deeper into the labyrinth
sheltered, a dome of branches
tangled stark, jig-sawing a pale sky.
A mattress of wet leaves redolent,
flecked with russet and ochre,
spreading over roots uncontained,
simmering in slatted light shafts.

There half sunk, half visible, apples
fallen and disowned lay scattered
pale and green and fresh,
shiny skins against dappled backcloth,
an arc of sunlight glancing them.
I open the mouth of my sack,
it was for the fruit that I came.

But the perfect curve deceives,
my fingers slip into black curd,
a rotting belly's mildew.
Too late, a second comer to the worm
and maggot, I recoil in disgust
leaving it to them empty, out of season,
gnawing relentlessly at the heart-seed.

Bee Song

Busy little bee
Busy little bee
Busy
Busy
Busy little bee

Busy little bee
Busy little bee
Little
Little
Busy little bee

Busy little bee
Busy little bee
Be Busy
Be Busy
Busy little bee

Busy little bee
Busy little bee
Be little
Be liitle
Busy little bee

Hide

Beneath the songs of two summers
he waited in a woven hide,
caged by twisted stems
and the forest surrounding him.
A hole made for two eyes, or one,
a camera, his second memory.

Elusive bird like a fading dream
or gem whose precious colour
drives him to this existence,
the living stillness of trees.
So he waits, patient for a visit
to release him from the call.

A shadow combs the clearing,
hovers, a life-time of instinct,
the crest inclined for sounds.
He freezes to a photograph,
focuses on a found moment,
beyond is green and distant.

In winter light, like leaves of autumn
a swan, pure-white is slowly landing.
Her sleek form now discovered,
the hand positions to record
and capture her forever but
withdraws, eyes rich with memory.

Capital

Circus

This is the quiet time.
A sun-filled evening fades
across a levelled lawn.
Far from the city I lie still
across two white chairs.
There is song from birds
calling through an open door.
In Oxford Circus people flow,
numbers I cannot imagine,
fill buses and fall asleep,
nameless on named streets.
At home in our woodland I
wander below shafts of light,
careless of where they led me.

Parliament

Foolish Icarus, so near to the sun
but ambitions burn at Westminster,
eternal on walls of gothic tracery,
your children descend with less grace.

Piccadilly

There is fever here,
very head is whirled round.
What carries them forward
is no steady pulse
but a law god gave to the lemming.

Clouds

Once we will remember when young
and lifeless on brilliant days,
when a bright sky-blue ceiling stretched
forever over sleepless grassy banks

And ghosts of continents drifted over us
above the tune of the silent earth.
When ticking watches died on our arm,
and birds migrated to another universe.

To understand these soft messages sent,
floating in white whirlpools, pale and
translucent, like whisps of heaven in a
slow masquerade, gently blowing over.

And see a hoary face, a hill, or wild hound,
running and fading to its own oblivion,
or the last breaths of a dying god,
above a city's roar, as traffic lights change.

40 Nights

Milk-white the moon
sheds her segment.
His door opens to
a desert wilderness.
With such innocence
he left grieving more
than his kingdom.

Keep

Rooks nestle here, black as cinders,
carry the history of the world
since it cooled. I startled these
huddled on a wind-blown parapet,
a flurry of wings sent them upwards
shrieking protests at my prying visit.

I came to admire stone's perversity
not birds, a stubborn will of defending,
barring granite teeth at tarmac advance.
Wars have changed their colours
swords given up, a scholar's promise,
the invisible enemy's soundless march.

Pilots like my father served here
from these rooms, listening to the air's
low drone, rocking uneasily in chairs
or leaning united, by the vast columns
tapering into swirls of pipe-smoke.
If sirens wailed the whole floor clattered.

Now old doors creak as the memory does.
I clear a window, a large rook arcs
into view, eyes me down a long beak
through the flame in his tiny coals.
All the openings are being walled up soon
to stop night visitors climbing in, or out.

Garden

When you call them in
you call the ghosts
from the darkest garden.
It is ours, doors open it.

Passing where we stand
a last breath draws in.
we shiver, tonight is cold
disturbed by their return.

Outside is black ocean where
eyes dance like silver fish
in pairs, thy grow before us
the ghosts come home.

Our cats are given back
from dark corners ungrown.
Their velvet coats bring night
and eyes shine with black sky.

The fire curls them to sleep,
we close the doors secure.
A touch leaves them to darkness,
and moons to gaze through us.

Pylon

Steel feet press heavy on the cornfield.
Over each harvest a tall shadow
offers beckoning arms to heaven,
straddling the flowering hedgerow,
watchtower of an alien legion
that invisibly raped but did not leave.
Crows settle on the lattice ribs
as if there was flesh to scavenge,
anxiously hopping to and fro
and finding it unexpectedly warm.

Awakening

Windowed moonless night,
a drawn curtain lifts
and falls
between two breaths
of my waking in
twilight of beginning.

Room-lit, a small universe
fills the grey,
furniture of growing.
Silk of sleep mirrors back
where I was here once,
a child of unknowing.

And before birdsong dawn
a chirp of time
separates the heartbeat
and ends
the ending of silence.
Hiccup of the stillborn.

Computer Crash

A world gone
blank where once
there were words

through a window
sky-blue opens
tops of ancient trees

as a blue screen
sucks time
to a singularity.

To press the key
fire-light
a silent living

while huddled heads
stare lid-less
in caverns of capitals.

December

Land of white,
as though
delicate hands
laid fresh down
like a careful mother
on angled roofs
of quiet cats

And cars on
driveways stayed
on driveways.

Fluff of streets
and in gardens
a child's shriek
punctures snow.

Under hoary leaves
branches lean,
bleached over
a new birdsong.

Daring to walk
on ashes of god,
breath smothering,
finger-chilled,
three score years
wrapped in
cold light of evening.

Bicycle

A firm grip on the saddle-back,
my father's hand gently push
at thin tyres wavering
in a drunkenness of self-doubt.

Just few rasping words
command wheels to align
and forward with jutting chin,
elbows angled, teeth clenched.

Stamping on stubborn pedals
roads narrow to an arrowhead
parades of houses fast forward
warm rubber hums the tarmac.

White lines pulse and break
under a whirring chain
send semaphores backwards
to a small silhouette hunched.

Repeating over and over, to
go home and climb the rooftop,
scatter the guffawing crows
and to the radiant sky proclaim,

"Rejoice, he is on his way!"

Father

Now I go your way
yard on yard
the step on soil

If stones turn
and dust is kicked
clouds swirl
and voids fill

So we move on
father and son
embraced in time

Bones outlive age
and earth reclaims
till we become
as we are
atoms of worlds.

Cake

Twenty five candles burn before me
with twenty five behind.
The rambling years and blank milestones
circle to an order not mine.
We are the measurer of all things
a quarter century, a silver wedding,
a year when ….
The cake is cut into equal portions,
a tap drips slowly in the kitchen.

Mother

All gardens surround you
where once were tended.
A house hollowed
still echoes there, where
flowers lifted from the sill.

I see you now and then,
in a darker sleep,
hunched in quiet labour
at the edge of neat grass,
painfully cutting green stems.

Twins

The................thing
with...............twins
..........is
that...............they
both...............come
.........from
the................same
egg................and
.........then
you................can
not................then
.........tell
which..............one
is.................which
.........but
we.................love
them...............both
.........the
same...............for
all................time

Fireworks (I)

A galaxy of stars,
here's one for you
they are powder in our hands,
stacked in the box
like dried cocoons,
roused from sleep with fire.
We leave the glow of our house
into the cloak of night
and the pearl moon's chill.

I shiver and lunge to light
the precarious touch-paper.
Spirits of the dead erupt,
they wail and scream
over tumbling laughter.
We shout and point at
constellations exploding
haphazard and volatile,
and beyond our reaching.

Fireworks (II)

They look so simple
in the shop
small cubes, sticks
and pyramids.
We put some carefully
in a box, like eggs
soon to hatch.
Tonight a garden glows
with orange flame,
our bonfire cracks
and snaps, red flames
threaten the moon,
our shadows gather
in a circle drawn
like moths to light.
Explosions crack night,
a rocket hisses
into bright light.
An umbrella of stars
fall to earth like
autumn leaves and
a faint smell of ash,
not yet dead.

Alfie

Cat o'nine tales
Garden sphynx
Ginger tom minx

Cat of nine lives
Pidgeon predator
Tiger furry bright

Cat with cat's-eye
Sneaker under gate
Hedgerow hider

Cat in the catkins
Bone maker
Stalker of starling

Cat on tin roof
Back archer
Silent stealth fighter

Catspaw stretcher
Baby-like cryer
Bin man hater.

Mosaic

Fragments are all you have
and time to place them
edge by edge. Rich colours
shine like jewels to your eye.

In the bleached courtyard
water splashed on stone,
a dancing fawn
carved in your childhood.

Your hands full of marble
feel their shapes betray you,
a picture incomplete and
weeping you run inside.

Your father saw you kneeling.
With a bag of coins
he leaves to buy you more,
for they will not match again.

Passengers

For the thirtieth time we round the bend,
the engine drags, levels then climbs.
Headlines burn back the darkness
spotlights forever, the hurtling road
under the bonnet's perfect metallic lip.
My knuckles whiten on the wheel
and your sleeping head nods
as if by intuition, we converse now.

You dream, running through large rooms.
I think only of our heat merging.
Outside scattered farmhouses,
caught in an endless net of fields
overlap and separate a fleeing horizon.
We move on, slicing headwind,
past eyes frightened under hedgerow,
bound to each other, breathing same air.

Perfume

An hour to midnight then a half-hour past,
sleep submits to counting as skin slackens.
Outside someone is running, a dull
thud approaches and fades, like a heart.

Daybreak clamours with a city's roar and
as reason tempts me from madness or love,
part awake, I think on a lover's fragrance
and lilac's sweetness in the tropical storm.

Beach

That one fine day
we ran back into
the sky-bue sea
under sea-blue sky
lived in a land of
pure white sand
where no one was rich
and no one was poor
and the young played
with the old
and the old played
with the young
with no fancy cars
or crappy ones
of any colour
and no fancy houses
or crappy ones
of any colour
no large or small
just me and you.

Dissection

Our hands lie apart
each finger flat
unmoved by distance
numb from cold
from a whiteless winter.
We are severed veins
The blood slows by degrees
to thin colour.
A blade between us
executes the healing.
The surgeon's hand
less steady than ours
now bathes in water.
We remain without mouths
only eyes, frozen
like two dried clots.

Gallery

Pictures hung where he would not enter
now, or kneel on pavements
to trace faint lines of her face lost,
knowing rainfall chased them to dreams.

Once in a long corridor of a hundred faces
he meandered amongst white statues
their colourless hue of purity,
staring eyeless and breathless in envy.

Celebration

Today was a Myday
A Happy Day

An I-think-of-you day
A run-skip-and-jump day

Oh through this week
heart-thumping
and kerb-kicking

Oh that this too, too
sunny face would
melt thaw
and dissolve itself

Oh how me conscious
pricks me bonscious!

(Gottya smiling sun
of spectrimized fulthrillment)

Yes it was a very Veryday
Happy Mirthday!

Not Gone

Bare hallway
with footfall
to leave
my love
but then
I heard
you stir
last night
your hair
burned gold
and red
twilight turned
to fire.

Rage

Bury me a hundred deep
fathoms or feet
it matters not which.

On a burning barge
my ashes take
windward over a forgotten lake.

Raise the homestead
pillage all crops
ransack the frail heart's hopes.

Lay me stark in the midday sun
I came this way once
I shall not come again

Shadow

My life-long brother is born without name,
he lives on the back of my heel.
We leave and return, yolked to a path
as I turn my eyes from the brilliant sun
towards his dark silhouette of gloom.

Persistently his hours orbit mine,
his mime is silent as the grave,
matching every deed that I perform,
a hinged-twin without a heart,
pursuer of everywhere I run.

His moods manifest in many shades,
blackness sharp as a knife,
then mellowing into cloud.
Belly-down he snakes towards me,
my back turned as the light fades.

Just A Game

Serve and return
Love fifteen
Umpire staring
Ace down the line

Love thirty
Top spin soft slice
Fifteen thirty feeling shirty

Umpire calls me
over to warn me
Makes me frown
Towel down sit down

Top spin ball
Back spin ball thirty all.
Feeling tall
Backhand
Forehand
Cross court smash
Now must dash
Thirty forty

Back to the baseline
Right side left side
Duece
Strings are pinging
Lob
Close to winning
My advantage
good at this stage

Line call 'no ball'
margins so small
Winner down the line
Umpire nods fine.
First set is mine, all mine.

Christmas Party

I kiss you a Merry Christmas
I kiss you a Merry Merry Christmas
I kiss you a Merry Merry Merry Christmas

And a Nappy New Year !

Typewriter

Typewriter typewriter typewriter typewriter

write typer write typer write typer
typer write typer write typer write

type type type type
write write write write

write typerwrite write typerwrite
type writertype type writertype

write type write type
type write type write

Typewriter typewriter typewriter typewriter

Backstage

Think back
Think back to back

Pat on the back
Cheers from the back
Front to back
Ride at the back

Queue at the back
Long at the back
Join at the back
Wait in the back
Short at the back

Seat at the back
Stay in the back
View from the back
Pain in the back

Noise at the back
Hide in the back

Man at the back
Girl on her back
'Give it back'
'Don't give it back'

Talk back
'Don't talk back'
Take back
'Don't take back'

Track back
Run to the back
Pack on the back
Don't look back

Stab in the back
Never coming back

Eight Thoughts

If you can paint a thousand words
Who needs writers?

If all world's a stage
Who's in the wings?

If you can't take a joke
Then don't take it.

If music be the food of love
Eat your heart out.

If you could turn back time
This never happened.

If I had a hammer
No one could nail me.

If I ruled the world
There would be no rulers left

If you are happy and you know it.
Good.

Planet

Planes in the sky
Trains on track
Ships on oceans

Trucks on tarmac
Cars in lanes
Feet on footpaths

Dogs on leads
Cats after cats
Birds on the wing

Ladies in lavender
Men on the moon
Kids on computers

Bees in honeypots
Swans on lakes
Flies in the ointment

Elephants in rooms
Snakes in the grass
Rabbits in headlights

Flowers in vases
Trees in the wind
Waves on beaches

Girls in town
Boys on beer
Soldiers in the field

Ash in urns
Love in the air
Earth round the sun

Choices

Which comes first?

The chicken or egg
Itch or scratch
A fly or my soup
Bathwater or the baby
Head or tails
Silence or the lambs
Love or hate
Sun or the moon
Pistol or sword
Moses or the commandments?

Which comes first?

Fish or chips
Spear or shield
The laugh or cry
Left foot or right foot
Face or the mirror
Something or nothing
War or peace
The green or red wire
Now or later
Save the women or the children?

Which comes first?

Bed or breakfast
Midday or midnight
Dry or wet
Agree or disagree
Life or death
Land or the sea
Boy or girl
Night or day
God or men
Spring summer autumn or winter?

Bladud

Father of Lear became prince of lepers.
Scorned in court,
he shuffled out
to drive pigs through marshes,
bones in rags,
stumbling after the meat.
Until one spring,
nosing for acorns
they all sank deep into the morass.
He waded in after
till chin-deep
but emerging, clean as a new pin.
So discovering a land
where miracles live in the mire.

Suspension

When Donald rose to heaven
he saw the sign
that the pearly gates were closed.

And the sign said unto him
after two thousand years
refurbishment was the holy orders.

Cracks in the paintwork needed filling
the white was off-white
railings rusted and new stairs needed.

An alternative place was available
below ground with open fires,
but he found the rooms too hot.

So he stayed midway, neither existing
or not.

Surveyor

Now is the hour of the leveller,
he paces slowly up and down our street.
Terraced house face each other
shoulder to shoulder, as if on parade
under the glare of the general's eye.
They are trembling at his footfall,
with foundations unsettling underfoot.
It is time to meet for all their maker.

No door is barred, he sees inside and out.
Surfaces that hide many sins,
paintwork, render, he burrows to the bones.
Old walls are condemned for new
where driving rain crept through
or water climbed like ivy from the soil.
Our little bays and shop windows of fancy,
where poorly built, will be pulled away.

In the dark musty corners of lofts
cluttered with boxes and dusty books,
gas masks, discarded toys and clothes
he hunts the resident rot and woodworm.
Our surgeon cuts away the canker
if roofs would crash onto sleeping heads
or floor yield plunging us to our doom.
The best are reborn, the worst go down

We lower the drawbridge at his trumpet call,
listen, listen he is riding through the gates.
Our king rules with a rod of iron
the rooms where we lived and loved.
Before God keeps us as tenants of the soil
houses feel new blood running through,
doors slam again, laughter from within.
The surveyor sees his children are well fed.

Money-Lender

He appears behind a wooden door
and leads you to his crooked desk.
He is the giver and forgiver,
with eyes as brown as pennies,
his teeth clatter like tumbling silver
while you squirm inside has grasp.
His words spill into your open cap
the lender acquires you by inches.

A single candle flickers in the gloom,
beads of sweat roll down your neck,
you bargain for charity, a plot
of freedom and he owns estates.
In the yawning vaults of his mind
rattling keys echo, locks turn
as he surveys his mountains,
nuggets of gold stacked to the rafters.

All you have are word and a dream,
immeasurable promises. It's facts, mate
facts. Speak to him in numbers,
your coins belong to the lender realm,
his smile is stamped on both sides,
heads he wins and tails you lose.
Your only home is a mortgage
and marriage is a merging of accounts.

Hunger for bread you shall be filled,
the bread-giver pulls loaves
like rabbits from a magician's hat.
So let him stay and lick his wounds
dealt by a scourging Nazarene.
Before his office turns back to temples
the lender may wear his laurels, ruling
a kingdom without boundaries or laws.

Tribute

Dickie Day
Dickie Day

used to

say history

repeats itself
repeats itself

every day

until he

passed away
passed away

one time

on a

Dickie Day
Dickie Day

Trenchman

I can still see one-eyed Wallie
with his cracked-earth smile
surrounding his baccy,
grey-white, angled by gravity.

Leaning steep on his shovel,
propping gentle on him
for as many years they can
recall, moving clay and drain.

He was master of the strata
and all that was surveyed,
a short body, brown-baked
in the red sun of his face.

Fingers roped the iron spade,
gouged glistening trenches
flat-bottomed, swill bled out
from innocent ground turned.

And as the curled shadow dies
his workday done, he unfurls
a patched, soiled sleeve
that the ground relentlessly tugs.

Sarcophagus

The lion that once roared inside
now sleeps at your feet, he has
turned to stone and will not turn again.
You remain, an eternal worshipper
last of a god fearing tribe.
The sculptor set your praying hands
towards heaven, you are his history too.

The long sword wheeled over hostile
lands, drove heathens from temples,
cleaved the skulls of idols,
as a compass over, points you east.
It is a restless sleep, eyes wide open,
willing your stone prayers
beyond vaults twisting into darkness

What if we cautiously lifted up, or
broke open, silence preserved so long?
A wrinkled mouth might speak
and send us reeling, truth turn to dust.
Effigies without hearts to outlive us,
they will share secrets, breaking like
a sigh, when we are gone for good.

Better to let the sleeping lie
than trespass veiled boundaries.
Besides it is late and shadows darken,
growing like fingers around us,
the devil's gaoler is stalking his prey.
We cross threshold and pause outside
breath in familiar air, uncertain years.

Churchyard

Rosebuds grow on silent graves,
to flower where tears shed,
or smother a cruel geometry,
cut deep in swaying greensward.

Island of garden and sepulchre,
for the fading of words,
hedgerow-hidden, where
starlings play by Sunday children.

If there is heaven in earth, it is here,
now, in glade and canopies
of brief cherry-blossom,
and by trees, or quiet fall of leaves.

With my shadow over your name,
not touching what was said
or unsaid, forever the visitor
to sun and shade across stone.

Remembered

They still live here

beyond the whistle at dawn
over the killing wires
out of an erupting earth

They still live here

within hollows of far fields
and red wildflowers
among a silenced village

They still live here

at footfall to front doors
after sunset and loss
within a short letter sent

They still live here

behind heart's ageing eye
in words on silent mouths
on pureness of white stone

They still live here